discovermore

Transportation

Focus on Cars

Doug Bradley

Britannica Educational Publishing

IN ASSOCIATION WITH

THE ROSEN PUBLISHING GROUP

Published in 2026 by Britannica Educational Publishing (a trademark of Encyclopædia Britannica, Inc.) in association with The Rosen Publishing Group, Inc.
2544 Clinton Street, Buffalo, NY 14224

Distributed exclusively by Rosen Publishing.
To see additional Britannica Educational Publishing titles, go to rosenpublishing.com.

Editor: Greg Roza
Book Design: Michael Flynn

Photo Credits: Cover Art of pixels/Shutterstock.com; (series background) Dai Yim/Shutterstock.com; p. 4 Dean Drobot/Shutterstock.com; p. 5 (left) Jakub Sisulak/Shutterstock.com; p. 5 (right) PaulLP/Shutterstock.com; p. 6 Gaschwald/Shutterstock.com; p. 7 Johnnie Rik/shutterstock.com; p. 8 Elena_Alex_Ferns/Shutterstock.com; p. 9 Vera Larina/Shutterstock.com; p. 10 Visionsi/Shutterstock.com; p. 11 udaix/Shutterstock.com; p. 12 loraks/Shutterstock.com; p. 13 Toa55/Shutterstock.com; p. 15 (top) https://commons.wikimedia.org/wiki/File:Fardier_a_vapeur.gif; p. 15 (bottom) https://commons.wikimedia.org/wiki/File:Capture_d%E2%80%99%C3%A9cran_2016-10-14_%C3%A0_21.26.28.png; p. 16 https://commons.wikimedia.org/wiki/File:1885Benz.jpg; p. 17 https://commons.wikimedia.org/wiki/File:Bertha_Benz_with_her_husband_Carl_Benz_in_a_Benz-Viktoria,_model_1894.jpg; p. 18 https://commons.wikimedia.org/wiki/File:DuryeaBrothers.jpg; p. 19 Aldo91/Shutterstock.com; p. 20 Karl Benz (1844–1929) mit seiner Familie.jpg; p. 21 Susan Montgomery/Shutterstock.com; p. 22 https://commons.wikimedia.org/wiki/File:Ford_assembly_line_-_1913.jpg; p. 23 IN Dancing Light/Shutterstock.com; p. 24 Martin Charles Hatch/Shutterstock.com; p. 25 Darren Brode/Shutterstock.com; p. 27 (top) Brandon Woyshnis/Shutterstock.com; p. 27 (bottom) Darunrat Wongsuvan/Shutterstock.com; p. 28 emirhankaramuk/Shutterstock.com; p. 29 Flystock/Shutterstock.com.

Library of Congress Cataloging-in-Publication Data

Names: Bradley, Doug, 1971- author
Title: Focus on cars / Doug Bradley.
Description: [Buffalo] : Britannica Educational Publishing, [2026] |
Series: Discover more: transportation | Includes index.
Identifiers: LCCN 2025027572 (print) | LCCN 2025027573 (ebook) | ISBN 9781641905428 library binding | ISBN 9781641905411 paperback | ISBN 9781641905435 ebook
Subjects: LCSH: Automobiles--Juvenile literature | Automobiles--History--Juvenile literature
Classification: LCC TL147 .B725 2026 (print) | LCC TL147 (ebook) | DDC 629.222--dc23/eng/20250818
LC record available at https://lccn.loc.gov/2025027572
LC ebook record available at https://lccn.loc.gov/2025027573

Manufactured in the United States of America

Contents

Getting Around in Cars

Think of all the ways that you, your family, and your friends get where you need to go. You may walk or ride your bike to school. Many people take a bus to school or work. Your parents may drop you off at a friend's house in your family's car. These are all forms of transportation, and cars are one of the most popular kinds.

Most families in the United States have at least one car. Many families have more than one.

Automobile technology has come a long way in a very short time. These two automobiles were made about 70 years apart.

Cars are also called automobiles or motor vehicles. Trucks and buses are motor vehicles, too.

It's hard to imagine what life was like before there were cars. That's how important they are. Cars have made it easy for people to travel within a city or across a continent. They've also affected how people live. Before, people could only work at jobs close to where they live. Cars now allow people to live farther away from where they work.

Consider This

Imagine if there were no motor vehicles in our world. How would life be different? What would stay the same?

Our Four-Wheeled Friends

There are many types of cars on the road today and they can look very different from one another. In fact, the main thing the different kinds have in common is that they all have four wheels, with some rare exceptions. In the past, most cars were open, without a fixed top. Now, most cars are closed, except for a kind of car called a convertible.

Some manufacturers make cars with three wheels! Needless to say, they aren't as stable as four-wheeled cars.

The muscle cars of the mid-twentieth century were wildly popular. Today, many people enjoy restoring them to their original glory and showing them off.

Two traditional styles of cars are coupes and sedans. A coupe has two doors and a small backseat. Sedans commonly have four doors and can seat between four and six people. When a sedan has a door in back that lifts, it's called a hatchback. Minivans and **SUVs** are popular with families because they're roomy and big. Sports cars are built low to the ground and don't always have backseats. They're fast and fun!

WORD WISE

SUVS, SHORT FOR SPORT UTILITY VEHICLES, ARE VERY POPULAR AUTOMOBILES. THEY ARE BIGGER AND USUALLY MORE POWERFUL THAN CARS.

The Basic Parts

All cars have a body, wheels, an engine, a steering system, and brakes. The body is the outer shell. Most auto bodies are made of steel, but some are made of strong plastics or fiberglass. The body is attached to a chassis. This consists of a frame that holds all the other parts of a car together.

Manufacturers make cars in a small range of colors. Some owners pay extra for fun colors, such as bright pink.

A car's hood is a large door that covers the engine and many other parts needed to give the car power to move.

A hood is located at the front of the car. The engine is usually located under the hood. (In some cars the engine is in the back of the car.) Some of the first automobiles had steam engines. Later cars were built with electric engines, but those cars couldn't reach high speeds. Electric engines were replaced by gas engines, but electric engines are making a big comeback because they are better for the environment.

Consider This

Why do you think electric cars are better for the environment than engines that run on gasoline?

Let's Get Moving

Most cars have an internal **combustion** engine. In this kind of engine, a mix of air and fuel enters a number of cylinders through valves. Inside each cylinder, a part called a piston compresses the air-fuel mixture. Then, the mixture is ignited by a spark plug, which gets power from a battery. This results in a tiny explosion that moves the piston back. Another set of valves opens to let the waste gases out of the engine. This process, called the four-stroke cycle, happens over and over again very quickly.

Car engines are connected to other systems, such as the fuel, exhaust, and electrical systems. Altogether, they make a one very complicated machine.

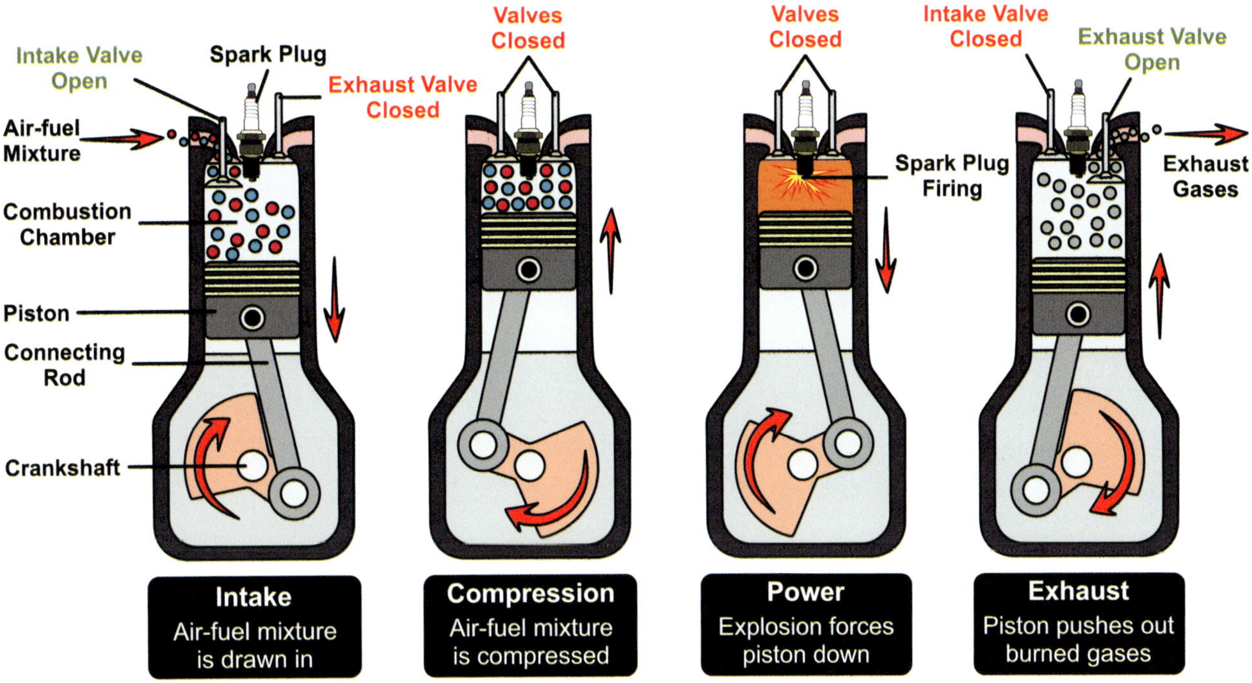

Pistons are attached via rods to the crankshaft. Parts connected to the spinning crankshaft send power to the wheels and other car parts.

The waste gasses created during the explosions are removed from the car through its exhaust system. A car's engine gets very hot, so a cooling system helps it cool down. The muffler cools the gases and reduces their pressure. Gas exhaust includes harmful chemicals.

WORD WISE

COMBUSTION IS THE PROCESS OF BURNING SOMETHING. IN INTERNAL COMBUSTION ENGINES, GASOLINE IS USUALLY THE FUEL BURNED TO MAKE POWER. ANOTHER COMMON FUEL IS CALLED DIESEL, BUT IT'S USED MOSTLY FOR LARGER VEHICLES.

The powertrain is the set of parts that send power from the engine to the wheels. The transmission is the part that controls how much speed and power the engine provides. A drive shaft carries this power from the transmission to the four wheels. Car tires are designed to keep a car from sliding on slippery or loose surfaces.

The transmission, also called a gearbox, uses a complex system of gears to change the speed and power the engine creates.

The large spring on this car is part of the suspension system. Without springs, every bump on the road would rattle drivers and passengers.

Brake pedals control the system that brings a car to a stop. When a driver presses the brake pedal, pistons send brake fluid through pipes to the brakes. The fluid helps move a part that pushes against the wheel to make it stop. Each wheel has its own brake. Wheels are attached to a car's suspension system. A suspension system has springs that absorb bumps.

Consider This

Think about how the different systems work together to keep the car in motion, help it stop, and make the ride safe and comfortable for passengers. Which system seems most important to you?

Developing Car Technology

Inventors first developed an engine that ran on steam in the late 1600s. The steam engine changed the world. It provided power for factories, mines, and railroads. It was also used in the first car. Nicolas-Joseph Cugnot of France built the first car-like vehicle in 1769. It was powered by a steam engine and had three wheels. Many companies produced cars that used steam engines during the later 1890s and early 1900s. One problem with the steam engine was that water had to come to a boil before the car could go.

During this same period, other companies built cars run by electric motors. Electric cars ran smoothly and were easy to operate. However, they did not run well at high speeds. Also, they could not go very far before the battery ran out and had to be recharged.

Cugnot is believed to have caused the first automobile accident in 1771 when he drove his new invention into a wall! The scene is depicted in this illustration from the early 1800s.

compare and contrast

Compare and contrast cars that used steam engines and cars that used electric engines.

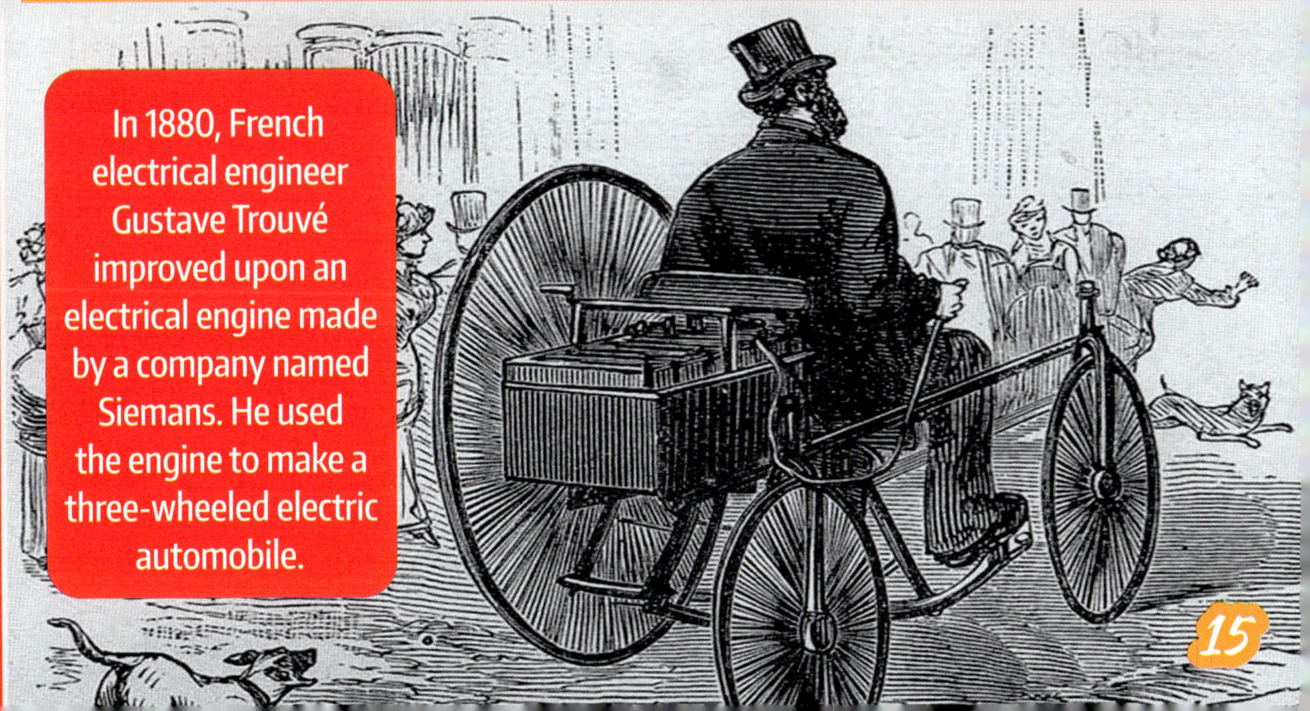

In 1880, French electrical engineer Gustave Trouvé improved upon an electrical engine made by a company named Siemans. He used the engine to make a three-wheeled electric automobile.

Karl Benz: Father of the Automobile

It wasn't until the gasoline engine was created that car technology became the focus of many inventors across the globe. Étienne Lenoir of France developed a gas-powered internal-combustion engine in 1860. Nikolaus Otto improved upon it in 1876. Around the same time, a German man named Karl Benz was tinkering with the gas engine, too. He also invented spark plugs, gear shifters, a water radiator, a clutch, and a battery-powered **ignition system**. By 1885 Benz assembled all of these parts into what many people consider to be the first true automobile.

The first Benz automobiles—which he called the Motorwagen—had three wheels and two gears. They were hard to control.

Bertha Benz drove 66 miles (106 km) during the first long-distance car trip. She made several suggestions to her husband based on her trip. She said the car needed more gears to get up hills. She is credited with inventing the brake pad.

Benz's vehicle had a gas engine and three wheels. Benz began selling his car in 1888. That same year, Benz's wife, Bertha, and her sons took a Benz machine on the world's first long-distance journey by car. The family's journey showed the world that cars were easy to use, and soon after automobiles became a more common sight in European cities.

WORD WISE

A CAR'S IGNITION SYSTEM STARTS THE BURNING OF FUEL INSIDE AN ENGINE. MANY CARS USE A KEY TO START THE CAR, WHILE OTHERS HAVE A PUSH BUTTON.

Early American Cars

Bicycle makers, brothers Charles and J. Frank Duryea, saw a gasoline engine at the Ohio State Fair in 1886. In 1891, Charles completed a design for a gas-powered, four-wheeled car. The brothers built it over two years. On September 22, 1893, in Springfield, Massachusetts, it ran successfully for the first time.

Charles and J. Frank Duryea pose in a car they made in this photograph from 1894.

Shown here is an early car from American inventor Henry Ford—the Quadracycle. Ford would go on to revolutionize the auto manufacturing industry.

The Duryea brothers' car was the first gas-powered automobile built and operated in America. In 1896, the Duryea Motor Wagon Company was the first car company to open in the United States. Other companies set up factories soon after.

Gas-engine cars were soon more popular than steam- and electric-powered cars. Cars became larger, faster, and easier to use. By 1910 carmakers started adding features that kept passengers out of the rain—including a folding-away top.

Consider This

Cars and bicycles are two forms of transportation that developed around the same time. How did they change the way people moved from place to place?

The Ford Motor Company

The car-manufacturing process was a slow and difficult one. Skilled craftsmen built cars from parts that were made by hand. Because of that, only wealthy people could afford to buy a car. This changed in the early 20th century thanks to Henry Ford.

Cars were so expensive to make that only the wealthy could afford them at first.

Henry Ford left a lasting impact on the car industry. Today, the Ford Motor Company is still a world leader in car manufacturing.

In 1899 Ford helped start the Detroit Automobile Company. The company focused on making cars to order for wealthy clients. He left the company and founded the Ford Motor Company in 1903. Ford had decided he wanted to make an automobile for the general public.

At this time, automobile manufacturers bought parts to build cars. Ford, however, wanted his company to make each and every part for its cars. He acquired iron and coal mines, forests, and mills to produce steel, fuel, wood, glass, and leather. He also bought railroad and steamship lines to transport his products easily. His efforts helped make cars more affordable.

Consider This

Why do you think that, by making his own parts, Ford was able to keep costs lower?

In 1908 the Ford Motor Company began producing the Model T. This car changed the world. It was sturdy and practical. Most importantly, it was cheap to make and cheap to buy because it was mass-produced.

Mass production is making things in large numbers to keep costs down. An important part of mass production is the assembly line. In an assembly line, a product is put together one piece at a time as it moves past workers on a belt. Each worker does just one task.

Shown here is a Ford assembly line from 1913.

So many Model Ts were sold that they're still around today. Many have been restored to their original state.

Ford didn't invent the assembly line, but he perfected it. His company used it for the first time in 1913. By the 1920s, Ford's assembly lines had produced millions of Model T cars.

The Model T was much more affordable than other cars. Many people were able to buy a car for the first time, and Ford's business boomed.

Consider This

How do you think life changed for average people once cars became affordable?

Growing Technology

Several other manufacturers were producing cars at the same time the Ford Motor Company helped bring cars to the mass public. Many of them, including Ford, operated in Detroit, Michigan. Detroit became the automobile capital of the world in the 20th century. Today, automobile manufacturing is still important in the area, but cars are made all over the world.

Germany's Volkswagen Beetle was an early form of compact car. It's still a popular car all over the world.

Some American manufacturers made fancier cars too. This was an alternative for wealthy drivers.

Cars have changed greatly since they were first invented. The first cars had no covering. They had a single seat, an engine, a steering device, and three or four large wheels. By the 1940s and 1950s American cars had become very large, but now cars come in many different sizes.

Modern cars have many features to keep people safe. Seat belts, air bags, and stronger frames keep riders protected if they are in an accident. Modern cars also have power steering, power brakes, automatic controls for windows and seats, and air conditioning.

Consider This

Can you think of any other improvements that have been made to cars since the early 1900s?

Cleaner Cars

Cars and other vehicles have had a harmful effect on the environment. This is mainly because gasoline produces harmful gases as it burns, which has caused widespread pollution on Earth.

Another problem with gasoline is that it is made from oil, which is a nonrenewable resource. That means that it cannot be replaced when it is used up. In the 21st century, some automakers have tried to solve this problem by making cars that use alternative energy sources. An alternative energy source is an energy source that cannot be used up.

Some cars run on biofuels, such as ethanol. Ethanol is a fuel made from corn oil. Other cars run on batteries. Hybrid cars run on a combination of gas and electric power. These cars are "refueled" by plugging in at charging stations. Charging stations were once hard to find and that limited how far people with electric cars could travel.

Large vehicles are usually worse for the environment because they use more gas than small cars and add more harmful gases to the air.

compareandcontrast

Gasoline and alternative energy sources are both used to power cars. Compare and contrast them and their effect on the environment.

Electric cars and charging stations have become far more common in recent years, allowing them to travel farther.

What's Next?

Today's cars have features such as **GPS** and cameras that help prevent drivers from hitting things. They are vastly different from the early cars that were manufactured over a century ago.

Can you imagine a car with no driver? Several car manufacturers are currently testing self-driving cars. The cars have cameras, radar, sensors, and computers that help them speed up, slow down, and stay in their lanes. The companies hope their self-driving cars will reduce accidents. They also hope that the cars will allow people who cannot drive to get around independently.

Car interiors are starting to look like airplane cockpits with all the controls, screens, and technology they now feature.

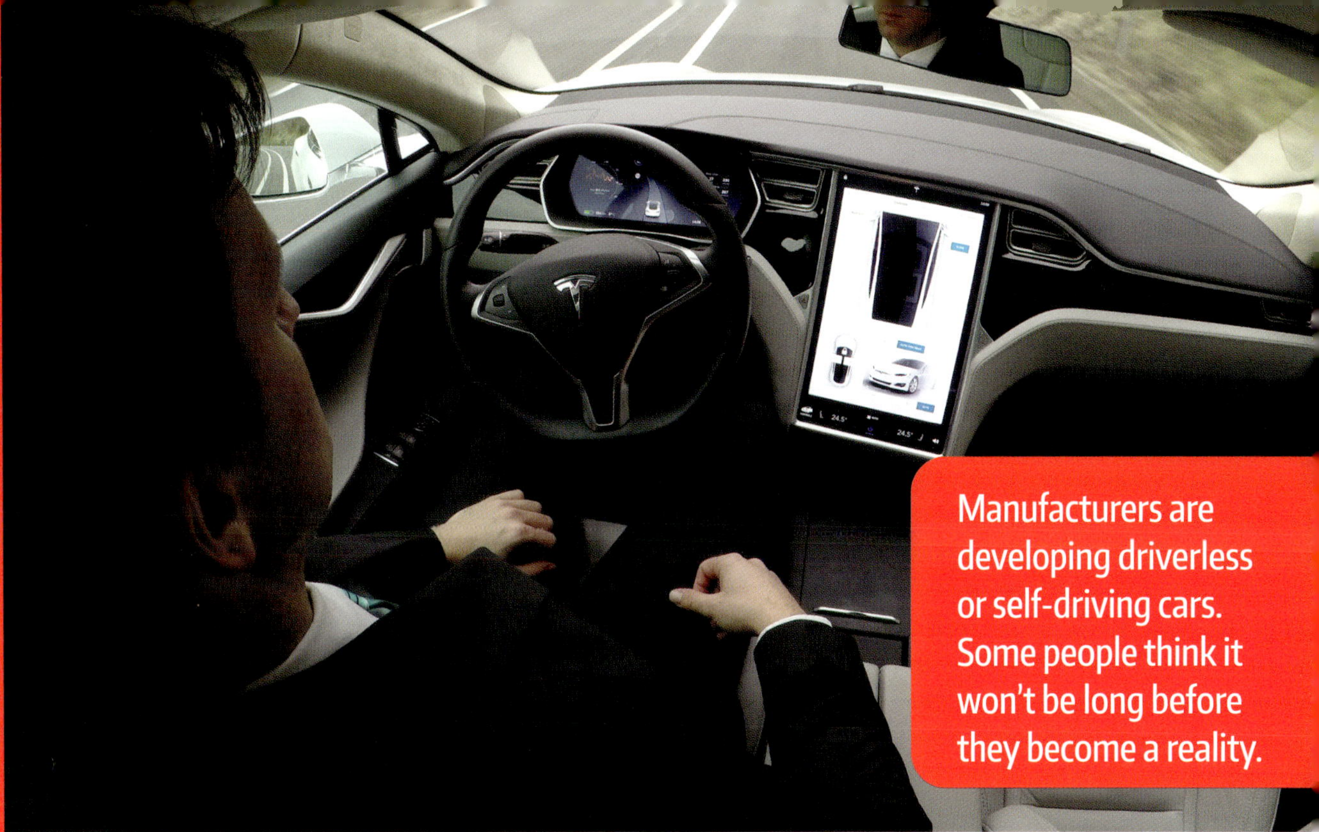

Manufacturers are developing driverless or self-driving cars. Some people think it won't be long before they become a reality.

There's no telling what the future of car technology holds. Maybe one day flying cars will be more than just science fiction. Maybe some cars will be able to drive on land and float in water. It will be exciting to see the next big development in car design.

WORD WISE

GPS IS A TOOL THAT USES SIGNALS FROM SATELLITES IN THE SKY TO HELP PEOPLE FIND THEIR WAY FROM PLACE TO PLACE. IT'S A PART OF MOST SMARTPHONES NOW. "GPS" STANDS FOR "GLOBAL POSITIONING SYSTEM."

Glossary

acquire: To gain.
biofuel: Fuel made from plant matter or animal waste.
chassis: A supporting frame, such as the body of a car.
clutch: In cars, a device that connects and disconnects the wheels from the engine.
cylinder: A long round hollow container. In internal-combustion engines, a part in which a piston moves up and down.
design: A sketch, model, or plan.
efficient: Capable of doing work without wasting time or energy.
environment: Having to do with the natural world` .
hybrid: A mix of things.
ignite: To set on fire.
manufacture: To make from raw materials by hand or by machinery.
nonrenewable: Unable to be replaced.
pressure: The force applied to something.
technology: The use of science to solve a problem and the tools used to solve them.

For More Information

Books

Dissected Lives staff. *Henry Ford Made Better Cars.* Newark, Delaware: Dissected Lives, 2022.

Fenmore, Taylor. *Look Inside an Electric Car: How It Works.* Minneapolis, MN: Lerner Publications, 2024.

Websites

Early Cars: Fact Sheet for Kids
www.si.edu/spotlight/early-cars
Read more about early cars and find a link to the Smithsonian Automobile Collection.

Fun Car Facts for Kids
www.coolkidfacts.com/car-facts
Read a fun collection of facts about cars and the history of cars.

Index